Elements

of

Fiction

Walter
Mosley

Grove Press
New York

3 9082 13964 7468

Copyright © 2019 by Thing Itself, Inc.

"Lying in a Hammock at William Duffy's Farm in Pine Island, Minnesota" from *The Branch Will Not Break* © 1963 by James Wright. Published by Wesleyan University Press and reprinted with permission.

FIRST EDITION

Published simultaneously in Canada
Printed in Canada

First Grove Atlantic hardcover edition: September 2019

Library of Congress Cataloguing-in-Publication data available for this title.

ISBN 978-0-8021-4763-9
eISBN 978-0-8021-4764-6

Grove Press
an imprint of Grove Atlantic
154 West 14th Street
New York, NY 10011

Distributed by Publishers Group West

groveatlantic.com

19 20 21 22   10 9 8 7 6 5 4 3 2 1

This book is dedicated to the memory of
John Singleton.

One of the most original and creative individuals
I have ever known.

Preface

This monograph is concerned with the hope of writing a novel that transcends story in such a way as to allow the writer to plumb the depths of meaning while, at the same time, telling a good yarn. It is not a manual offering prescribed steps that will inevitably lead to the writing of the perfect story. Rather, the intent of this essay is to explore the internal makeup of the elements of fiction writing. These elements are, among other things: character and character development, plot and story, Voice and narrative, context and description, content and the blank page and, of course, intentional structure versus vast troves of unconscious material.

Considering the goal of this essay and the nonlinear relationships of the elements of fiction, I have decided to approach the subject in a contemplative rather than a systematized form. That is to say, I do not believe there is a road map to Successville in fiction writing. There is no consistent rule to measure the level of achievement. Even if the author is happy with her work that doesn't mean she has done her best. Beginning, middle, and end are meaningless if you aren't, at least in some small way, breaking new ground.

For the serious writer these challenges may seem capricious, erratic, and intimidating—like some unfamiliar opponent in a combat ring of their choosing. The goal of the writer in this contest is the survival of the story in its ideal form. The goal of the story is the impossible brass ring of freedom. Neither rival can achieve absolute victory but they can fail—in some cases spectacularly.

Luckily for us and our work, failure is an essential raw material from which our stories arise. Failure encompasses the negative spaces of our tales; it guides us, teaches us, it loves our intentions better than any ambition. Failure makes our stories stronger while allowing humility to flow in our hearts.

Fiction is one of the few constructive human activities in which we have the potential to make something from almost nothing. Something from nothing. That kind of alchemy is a recipe for failure and also the hope for the miraculous.

When I say nothing I mean there is little to no physical material used in the creation of our tales. The *author* might just be an elder making up a story about a wolf and a little girl for the grandchildren on a rainy day when the larder is low. All the storyteller needs are words, imagination, and love—not necessarily in that order. These materials have a scant physical *footprint.* The story told might change every day, and the children might, probably will, remember a very different fable.

Something from nothing.

The plentifully available natural resources for fiction are found in language and the capacity for inarticulation, the senses and their continual reevaluation of the world we live in and imagine, and experience, which we glean from both conscious and unconscious sources, through reliable and unreliable recollections.

There's one last thing to say before we get into the main body of this disquisition, and that is—*condensation.* Even though I haven't used this word in the main body of the text, it is a major unspoken element of fiction writing. That's how you write a novel: you take a small section of the larger world (for example, retired cop culture in Saint Louis) and then crush the subject down to only those elements that are salient to the story being told. Once you've achieved this end you add as little of the commonplace as possible to make a story that seems large and real and pedestrian and, hopefully, revealing. The middle-aged ex-cops of Saint Louis become the readers' entire world—as large as, larger than, their minds can comprehend at any given moment. That's what our experience of the world is. Good novels are the same.

Introduction

Some years ago I published a monograph entitled *This Year You Write Your Novel*. It was meant to show the layman what the structure of a novel might be in its simplest form and also where content comes from and where it belongs.

In *This Year* I gave the simplest bases for novel writing. I said to write each and every day, to decide on a point of view to tell your story, to understand the concepts of metaphor and simile, plot and story, character and character development, and the importance of language, poetry, and, of course, the fact that writing itself was the act of rewriting.

That essay had moderate success and many writers and aspiring writers have told me that it gave them structure and some hope that their writing goals might be within reach. A few writers even said that they finished their first novel in part due to the advice they received.

I don't know how accomplished these first novels were, but that doesn't matter much. The act of writing a novel organizes the mind. It sends us on a journey that is uniquely personal. Also, if the writer has been diligent and honest with herself, she might very well be on the way to crafting a distinctive Voice that has the potential to reveal the world in new ways.

I'm pretty happy with *This Year*. It accomplished a goal. Now whenever anyone asks me how to write a novel, I just direct them to this monograph, confident that therein is everything important I know about that question—in its most basic form.

It is important for me to say here that *This Year* is not everything one needs to know about novel writing but rather it's a good start, mapping out the main avenues that the fledgling novelist has to be familiar with. But there are many unnamed side streets and shortcuts, wild detours and journeys to uncharted territories, and even undiscovered continents of thought. There are places and states of mind the novelist can discover that have never been seen, heard of, or imagined. Sometimes these undiscovered destinations seem at first to be familiar: a street-corner bodega or a country road, a comfortable bed or a doorway. In these seemingly common places the novelist might jolt us with strange revelations: guilt that we've never experienced or an interpretation of the ordinary that stands everything we've ever believed on its head. Like: A young boy's first wet dream. Your perfect father coming home drunk and violent. Death. A stranger waiting on the other side of that door who holds your future in her hands.

Some novels change the rules from the onset, depositing us on different planes of existence, making us into animals or aliens or the enemy we've always feared and despised. We might be wedged into the point of view of a paraplegic or someone who is deaf or blind. Or, on the other hand, we might experience preternatural, otherworldly senses that give us knowledge and sensations unavailable to anyone else—except, of course, our readers.

We may discover characters in our writing that speak from the unique genius of their culture opening new avenues, delivering us to places that the reader may have never imagined.

To create novels of this magnitude we have to dig deep inside our own hearts and minds, into our true histories and a future so definite that it may as well be our past.

The potential of novels to reveal what was previously unimaginable is so vast that I don't believe any manual or reference book, road map, field guide, or library could exhaust the possibilities. How does one, for instance, become a great predictive genius like Jules Verne? A writer who foretold the major scientific advances of the following century; an explorer who didn't have to leave his writing desk to see worlds invisible, impossible to almost anyone else.

Or we might consider a different kind of voyager— Herman Melville: a writer of such modernist sensibilities that his books can stand next to or above any literary work of any age.

How did these writers, and so many like them, pierce the veil of convention and create works of such power and individuality that their books might be thought to have lives of their own? This is the question that many writers have and few, if any, answer completely. We all have a piece or two of the puzzle somewhere in the depths of our souls; our souls where the passionate heart and the structured mind intersect. In this essay I will try to present one jigsaw piece that I have a tentative hold on.

The Structure
of Revelation

There was a phrase I used in *This Year* to explain the purpose of plot. I asserted that *plot is the structure of revelation.*

I find this interpretation useful inasmuch as it is both pedestrian and extraordinary. Simply said, plot is the construct or prism through which the story is revealed. *She's my daughter, she's my sister, she's my daughter,* said the Chinatown script. *The killer is . . .* , Nero Wolfe tells us at the very end of every Rex Stout book—and usually he's right.

In *The Plague,* by Albert Camus, we are presented with the carnage wrought by modern-day bubonic plague (a metaphor for war). We see the worst sides of humanity, while social institutions slowly disintegrate. It isn't until we're far into the book that we discover that the mildest, most hapless of the characters is destined to become the hero of the story. This slowly evolving reveal is designed to show us that there has always been hope, even in the darkest moments; and the potential for that hope resides in all of us, no matter our foibles, shortcomings or even our cowardice.

If we chose the right moment to reveal a truth about the story, we might create an epiphany for the reader that is striking, maybe even life altering. And yet the potential for epiphany is a minor benefit compared to the trace elements that come slowly to awareness during the unveiling of the story being told.

Plot isn't the only province of revelation. Indeed, the structure of the story itself may play but a minor role in the revelations brought about by the novel. Character is so important that often the people populating the novel carry more weight than the tale. Huckleberry Finn, for example, or Iago, Dexter, Sherlock Holmes, or Madame Bovary all end up towering above the stories from which they arise. And it's not only living, breathing characters that plumb the depths of understanding. Architecture, the weather, and geology all can be imbued with personality, life. As we get to know these places and structures, they start to have presence and meaning, purpose, and even character beyond their abstract, inanimate qualities.

And so, coming back to the phrase *structure of revelation*, I find that we can meditate on different kinds of structures and reveals; our writing has the potential to show different ways we can make our work transcend itself, bringing new and different truths to the fore.

These truths are in plot, character, physical appearance, place, ideas, and time as it passes.

What Is Structure in Fiction?

Before the pen touches paper there is nothing: an empty page both dumb and bristling with the intense desires of the would-be writer. That blank page or screen represents all the pent-up, unexpressed hope and knowledge harbored within us. We experience a powerful urge to speak, a longing akin to an infant struggling to express her deepest feelings: Mother. Hunger. What is that scary thing?

Like the aspiring writer, the toddler doesn't immediately have the right words to tell her story. But unlike the writer-in-waiting the little one doesn't have a consistent concept of giving up. She may get frustrated now and again. But as a rule she just keeps throwing sounds out there, along with gestures, physical contact, and facial expressions. She gets frustrated and then laughs, rolls around on the floor, and then maybe takes a break wondering about the fly that just landed on her nose.

Each one of these experiences becomes a part of the child's yet-to-be-told story. Tumbling is something like laughter. The tickle of the fly's feet on her nose causes laughter. The frustration is anger that you, the audience, cannot understand her attempts to communicate.

When words finally come to the child they spill out, seeking cohesion and finding infinite pleasure in explaining how rolling down a grassy hill makes the world a great jumble filled with birds and bumps, blue sky and green earth, dizziness, and then the laughter that makes it all worthwhile.

These are the primary elements of the structure of fiction. Seemingly unaffiliated experiences that come together under a single point of view. Story doesn't start out as structure but slowly assembles itself into a tale filled with surprises, comparisons, and resolution.

The child that became us is that desire to tell a story, because in the telling there is both survival and the proof that we exist. And it isn't only rolling around and wondering about clouds and bugs and gravity. Sometimes the young mind must fabricate logic to deal with the unimaginable: unsated hunger and monumental threat, abandonment and death.

*   *   *

I use the child-mind to begin the discussion of *the structure of revelation* because fiction and art in general are mostly instinctual, unconscious endeavors. Certainly there is a good deal of craft in creating revelatory moments in your writing, but that is only mechanics. Discovering what is important to both the story and the reader comes from that tumble down the grass hill. What I mean to say is that the child, the child-mind, instinctively understands that the world (in our case the novel) is larger than your head, your conscious experience.

The Blank Page

And so we return to the blank page, which represents, for so many, fear of the unknown . . . and what we might find there. Also, I believe, it calls up the basic fear of all creatures, that of nothingness, unknowing, death.

My advice when it comes to the first steps into emptiness, that moment when you embark on the self-revelation of the Word, my advice is that you approach it as a child would—that is, full of wonder and a sense of play. You have a keyboard and a blank screen, a pencil and a pristine sheet of paper. These are the toys. Get used to them. Start putting down words.

> I could only see the tiny head barely breaking the surface of the water. But I knew the turtle's huge body hovered underneath . . .

A memory, an idea, an ideal. Maybe you are that turtle. Maybe the turtle is your patron deity patiently awaiting your revival.

Maybe these words will lead you somewhere. Maybe they'll be discarded the next moment. It doesn't matter. What matters is that the emptiness is challenged by concepts and images trying to open a door to your story; trying to reveal some subject, some pathway to the mountain that will rise under you, bringing with it the truth that was forgotten in words crafted by your desires and your faithfulness to the child who has always needed to understand and explain.

Most beginning writers I've known believe in a kind of preordained structure to fiction. After all, they've read great writing like *The Metamorphosis* and *The Grapes of Wrath*, *Their Eyes Were Watching God* and *Dhalgren*. All these stories are uniquely told and they are structured in ways that reach beyond the mundane into the experience of the human heart and sometimes even into the soul. In the structure of great literature there seems to be no vestige of sweat, strain, or uncertainty, as beauty, fear, transcendence, and that singular vibration that is wholly human arise from these tales. We experience the language itself as a kind of Truth that calls to us, giving knowledge that will brook no petty dissent.

Who in their right mind would attempt to write anything close to these deep excavations into the human experience? How does one dare to compete with masterpiece?

The answer to these questions is: the child and the blank page.

When the child experiences an image or a story that touches his heart, he laughs or reaches out in wonder. The next minute or moment or day she celebrates that joy on the blank page.

"I feel sun in my tummy," he might write.

> It comes out of my fingers and my toes. It goes everywhere and takes me with on a big blue wagon that has a cowboy horse and big red wheels made from fire that didn't burn . . .

I am not young enough or innocent enough to use just the right language of a child, but I hope you can see how it seems to me that the child is not competing with or even imitating his experience. He is rejoicing in the gift given through the materials of his experience.

The blank page becomes a celebration of the beauty we have been shown by great writing, great art, and the extraordinary displays of nature.

So the first impediment and biggest obstacle to our novel, the blank page, becomes a big blue pond at dawn. All we have to do is jump in and flail around, laughing and discovering.

Is that great art? No. Art is not equivalent to a momentary whim or caprice. And yet, contradictorily, you cannot have art without whimsy. You cannot dance without stumbling now and then. You cannot build the story without mastering the tools the way children learn to play and speak—by discovering the truth while telling it.

The blank page is the writer's friend. It is an invitation to discover the words that will guide you to the story. You may already have a good idea of what your story should be: the blank page will help you sculpt that idea into something real. You might have no idea of what will come from your writing. All you know is that there was a field somewhere that once bore wild strawberries and now it's a parking lot. You feel that story and through the blank page you will deliver it.

The Novel Is Bigger than Your Head

Another obstacle the serious novelist almost always encounters is the loss of control in the face of his or her own story. There's so much going on that even the slightest change of character, detail, or plot might well turn the movement of the novel in a direction that could transform everything.

Maybe this tale started out as the account of an unhappy mother and housewife in Brooklyn, circa 1918. The war was over, and it returned to her a brute who was once her husband. Her children are confused and unhappy. Her job has been abruptly taken away and given to another vet who needs her to train him. She will soon lose all her work friends and is falling in love with the vet she's helping, while being beaten and raped almost nightly by the man who swore to *love and to cherish* her.

It's a hard story but a good one. It might even be an important chronicle detailing the roots of the issues that have dogged American women, all American women, even now, a hundred years later. It is a story blessed with a quality of simplicity that will allow many different kinds of readers to appreciate it. In the writer's mind, this is a novel that can almost write itself.

But as the writer sits down to the desk day after day, problems slowly begin to rise from the depths of story.

How can we justify this woman using feelings for one vet to free her from another? Isn't this the very servitude that started this hapless plight centuries before her birth? What about the crimes her husband commits against her? What about a society that won't even put a name on these offenses? What about the children, their characters and personalities, and their impact on the mother? What about her friends? What role do they play in this drama that seemed so simple just a week earlier?

And what about this war-battered working-class husband who has a condition that didn't have a useful diagnosis a hundred years ago? What about a society, a culture, a legal system that believes men are superior to women in almost every way?

Who is our main character? Do we want to define her by her victimhood? Her name is Sharon. Sharon's father died before she was born. Her mother, Lottie, had a female companion named Ilse. Sharon left home at fifteen, married Max Tourneau, and set up a new home for him and their kids.

Suffrage is on the horizon. Murdering Max is not out of the question. Her new lover, Pete, is a little kinky and she likes that . . .

But how can Sharon have a new lover while being assaulted by her husband? Maybe she starts drugging Max. Maybe Pete brings over the laudanum-laced gin, toasts Max, and then, while Max is unconscious, makes love to his wife.

Is this the Sharon we want to see? Maybe not. But how can a person living in the muck stay clean?

Sharon's story is only a small part of a much larger world. While she is loving Pete, as Max snores, Ilse, her dead mother's lover, is taking care of the children, under the impression that Sharon has gotten a job on the night shift at a cardboard factory. Sharon's oldest son, Paul, is dedicated to a father he's never known. Paul slips out of Ilse's house and makes his way through the dangerous city to get back home to Max—who suffers night terrors from the war.

What drives Paul? What were the nighttime streets of Brooklyn (and maybe Manhattan) like in 1918? What does Paul see and how does he respond?

These questions arise from the dramatic interplay between characters influenced by the times and also by their unique natures and experiences. Just these relations, associations, and affairs make for an unwieldy voyage on an endlessly turbulent sea of humanity. Keeping these elements running smoothly is not really possible. Even the narrative voice of the tale comes into question.

When you began this story it was meant to be a series of journal entries written by a barely literate Sharon. Maybe she intended them as instructions for her daughter to live a life that isn't oppressed like hers.

Hey! Maybe Sharon's great-granddaughter, Charlotte, is reading this journal in the late twentieth century on the eve of her wedding . . . No, no.

At its onset this novel was going to be told in a first-person narrative that would allow the beleaguered Sharon to have an outlet. But now we see that Ilse, Paul, and maybe even Max need points of view in order for the reader to understand what almost no one else can at this time.

OK then, it's settled: We'll use the third-person narrative voice with the major concentration on Sharon to tell the story of a woman in a world spinning out of control. This will be difficult. The story is already so large that almost every morning you are surprised by what your characters are saying and thinking, and things are happening that you didn't expect.

But the story is there. Will Sharon murder Max? Will young Paul stab Peter in the back? Will Ilse take the children away to some early twentieth-century health commune? It's not clear yet, but we're getting there.

You have character, story, plot, intense emotional and dramatic dialectic interaction, narrative voice, and an intention to reveal an experience handed down from generation to generation, epoch to epoch. It's perfect. A little bit bigger than your head (conscious mind) but manageable. You go to sleep looking forward to the next writing session, where everything, you expect, will come together.

You wake up to the late spring's early sun. This light fills your bedroom. Maybe someone is breathing next to you, still asleep. There's a child down the hall and a parent living a few blocks away, laboring under the weight of early emphysema.

You remember the line from Emily Dickinson, "A light exists in Spring." The world, different from any other time, comes together under that light becoming all of a piece. It is a beautiful phrase, and you lie there with it for a while, happy to exist within something so beautiful.

Then the shadow of a thought intrudes. The fact of that spring light is also a fact of fiction. Something has to hold it all together. Sharon? Yes, but not really. New York? Only inasmuch as the story has to unfold somewhere. A woman's predicament? Yes. But this light is still only diffuse in your novel; it has no direction, nothing for it to illuminate or reflect upon. And then you remember *suffrage*: a strong wind raging toward freedom. Suffrage: an abrasive, loving, demanding, uncompromising voice that calls out and shouts down beliefs that have been held for centuries. Suffrage that echoes the word *suffering*, which in turn is Sharon's bitter life.

Yes, of course, you have character, story, plot, dialectics, narrative voice, and an intention to reveal; but the fiction you're writing, the novel that attempts to transcend mere story into meaning, also needs context.

Context

Context is the world we inhabit, the light of morning, children, belief in God, or maybe it's a hunt or an escape, a passion or an emptiness so profound it can be filled only by death.

Melville's context was the ocean and a great white whale. Dickens had the poorhouse. Many of Mark Twain's tales had us navigating the Mississippi River with both intention and abandon. Context. Suffrage.

With this thought the world and the complexity of your novel increase exponentially. Max's rages have an object and a subject. Pete is reduced to a peter. And the children become the heirs of an age. Ilse is an unheralded prophet. Sharon may narrate most of this story, but she won't understand, not completely. And you, the writer, are saddled with a humongous problem. How do you include this universal struggle for equality without becoming didactic, allowing politics to overwhelm the fiction? The moment you and your story are overwhelmed by the furious storm of the times— that's when the real novel begins.

When Sharon's husband found himself in the hell of war, he gave up, accepted death—but didn't die. When he got back home and visited that hell on Sharon, she despaired. And so on. That echoing magnitude is your novel and you writing your novel. The answer is in the writing, not your conscious mind. Like that child throwing herself into the pond, you throw yourself into this story, letting it toss you and your characters about like detritus in a whirlpool.

The novel is bigger than your head, and it should be. Years after it is published some reader, some critic will pick it up and see things that are there but that you never intended. The revelations, reverberations, and echoes of good writing go on forever—or at least for a very long time.

Character

Character presents the lens or lenses through which the novel is experienced. Our protagonists' thoughts and encounters are doorways to the new world of the novel. These actors see their environs and talk about them; sometimes they even understand what it is they say and see. In a way character is synonymous with journey, because every important player moves within and is transformed by the story told. Though fictional, our characters are experienced by readers as blood and bone, heart and mind, good and evil people who attract and repel them, remind them of something or someone or an experience that offers us a deeper, and deeper, understanding of the world we're all immersed in, while at the same time carrying vital information about the *real* lives we are living, have lived.

Character is a beast of burden. It carries our food and tools, our weapons and journals, our dreams and desires, along with all the bits and bobs that accumulate over a lifetime: The locket taken from Aunt Harriet's body because Adaline feared that some other family member would steal it. The photograph secretly taken of the woman who lived across the street, the woman Steven never had the courage to speak to.

In this way character is also history. We know the people in our novel, like everyone, are lifelong collections of experiences, both conscious and unconscious. The only difference with these characters is that we can see further into their hearts and know more of what they think and say than we'll ever know of their living, breathing counterparts in the *real* world.

> Mama Lorenzo told Holland that his brother's new bride, when she was four, spent the afternoon at the house of a man who was later convicted for child molestation.
>
> "We just hope to God that Mr. Milo was decent that day," Mama says.

This brief encounter, this painful confession, is something you might never know about your own spouse or in-law. The novel can use its many players and their multifaceted points of view to create a greater breadth of knowledge than most mere mortals have access to. The narrative voice of the novelist carries authority that in many ways is more revealing than any other medium—including film.

The potential of the narrative real estate the writer controls is obvious, but this power can also be a hindrance to good fiction. Sometimes we load up our players with knowledge and understanding that they don't really have access to. Sometimes, instead of revealing a truth, we simply have one of our players say it or act it out. Our beasts of burden can carry a tin skillet, but that doesn't mean they can prepare a mess of grits; they exist in a world of sublime articulation, but they themselves often have little idea of what transpires in that world.

And so we have it. The character is much like a great boxer in his prime. He can bob and weave, has knockout power in either hand, has extraordinary endurance, but for all that he is cursed with a glass jaw. Therefore his abilities have to be used judiciously, because even just a well-placed jab could negate all that he has accomplished.

Revelation for and through character is one of the major, and certainly most irreplaceable, pillars of your novel. What our hero learns, or fails to learn, touches our hearts; it drives us as it goads the protagonist down the often awkward journey of life. From love to loss. From innocence to truth. From the clean lines of revenge to the transcendence of forgiveness.

Character Development

I have writer friends who spend a great deal of time outlining and detailing the biographies of their major characters. Through this process, I am told, they discover the motivations underlying actions taken by these players as they move across the stage of the novel. This may very well be a powerful and productive way to construct an Iago or Sister Carrie. It is, however, not my way of discovery. I meet my characters the way I encounter people in life—at a place and in a situation where I have less knowledge than I'd like and am almost always, at first, paying attention to the least important details. After that, I'm in *discovery mode.*

I mention the biographical approach to character development because some writers feel more comfortable forearmed with the knowledge of personal history. I see where this approach can be both useful and pacific. If you know the education, age, sexual preference, family history and much of the minutiae of a person's life, your decisions (and theirs) will be more accurate and possibly less distracting.

So if you, my fellow writer, find character bios useful, then by all means use them. Because the creation of a novel is akin to a mad scramble up a mountainside layered with loose pebbles. Any handhold or solid ground you can find will be a blessing.

That said, there is no preordained pathway to your ultimate destination. You may know everything about your protagonist's life from insemination to her degradation by worms in the ground. But you will find that this creation of yours has a will of her own and she will encounter other well-defined characters who might force her to change direction and fly in the face of your deft templates and well-laid plans. In other words, she may not be who you thought she was.

Regardless of what you know before embarking on the novel proper you will have to discover, or rediscover, your characters in the prose of the work.

"Will you join me in a nightcap, Mr. Harmony?" Lady Estridge asked, the blue of her eyes echoing the pale hue of her teardrop diamond earrings.

"Not me, ma'am," the man calling himself Hurston Harmony replied. "I never drink or smoke, or eat the flesh of animals for that matter."

The slightest of smiles crossed the young heiress's lips. She nodded briefly and then led him from the garden courtyard into the library, where her uncle waited.

My attempt in this romance dialogue knockoff is to begin the discovery of two characters who may or may not be central to the story that has yet to unfold. The lady might be from the upper classes, while Hurston's language marks him as coming from more common roots. Her attention to detail, down to the color of her jewelry, is probably an accurate reflection of her aesthetics. Her smile is enigmatic, as is the placement of her uncle. Harmony might not be the man's name, and so his profession to being a vegetarian teetotaler may also be fabrication.

In this way we are set up from the start to have the intentions of three characters revealed. We probably expect some kind of con job. Maybe, if familiar with the genre, we might be looking forward to a sexual romp. We'd like to know what the date is. It could be the turn of the twentieth century or earlier. But when we find that the man calling himself Hurston is black and Lady Estridge is Kurd, then we might want to move the calendar up a century or so—or not.

My objective is to discover characters as they dive into the story looking to achieve their own ends and either finding themselves somewhere other than they expected or discovering that they had no idea what their goals would bring them. Maybe Mr. Harmony and Lady Estridge will, in spite of all their intentions, find love . . . even as it slips away.

So, in the case of Lady Estridge and Mr. Harmony, the story is the beard for the plot. It presents characters practiced in the sleight of hand of sophisticated repartee while at the same time having very serious hidden agendas that may or may not meet our expectations.

Somewhere there's a war going on between the Blue and Yellow armies, we learn. Lady Estridge's aunt's husband, Dieter Sandler, supplies the Blues with "materials such as blankets and freeze-dried foods. But never weapons, sir, never. It's against my religion."

He also points out that a great general of the Yellow Army is named Harmonious.

"Any relation?" he asks Hurston.

"Luckily, no," Hurston replies. "You are aware that any individual closely related to the Yellow ruling class is arrested, tortured, and held for ransom."

"Torturing a color," Ariel Estridge comments. "Sometimes I think that God created women but the Morningstar made men."

"Blasphemy!" Dieter exhorts.

This discussion contrasts the conflict between the Yellows and the Blues to the war of the sexes. It is there to reveal the elements of the age and the issues our characters must face. Though this banter and the danger and sexual tension prepare us for character development, they do not, on their own, achieve this end.

Character development requires change. It calls for transformation, literal transmogrification—both change and the process of change.

Let's say that Dieter has been appointed to be the conservator of Ariel Estridge's inheritance until she reaches the age of thirty-five. He is also, secretly, a high-ranking official in the intelligence bureau of the Blues. Hurston, who has proven himself a coward, tells Ariel, in private, that he has seen the document allowing Dieter to keep her from her birthright. All she has to do is marry and the contract is broken. If Ariel agrees to pay Hurston (whose real name is Jack Morgul) a 3 percent fee, he will marry her and then, after the three-year period mandated in the conservatorship agreement, he will divorce her.

Ariel detests Hurston and deeply respects Dieter but mostly she craves financial freedom.

Character Relationships

Ariel is also infatuated with a man named William Atherton III. Bill is a lovable sort. He rides horses and fights in the war, "like any real man, unafraid to face the finality of death."

Bill hates Hurston (Jack). So do Ariel and Dieter. But Ariel agrees to marry Jack because he shows no interest in her except for the 3 percent. She likes Bill but doesn't want that kind of family life right now.

There's only one catch: Jack must marry Ariel under his legal name. They do wed, spending their wedding night in separate beds. Ariel has no respect for Jack but he's oddly chivalrous and he cleans up after himself—a trait she greatly appreciates. He makes no demands beyond his 3 percent fee, and when Ariel falls ill he sits at her bedside for six days, bathing her with alcohol to keep the fever down.

Ariel thinks that Jack wanted to keep her alive for her money. Maybe she's right.

While she languished Dieter used all of his power to discover the details of Jack's origins. Dieter will lose a great deal of income after his conservatorship ends. He doesn't steal from Ariel but he uses his power of investment to curry favor with bankers.

While Ariel is recuperating it is revealed that Jack has a second cousin (by law) who is related (also by law) to a Yellow war hero—not a high-ranking official, just a brave soul who gave his life in battle. Jack is arrested. Dieter Sandler is assigned to interrogate him; Bill Atherton begins to court Ariel. Bill had rejected Ariel's friendship after her mercenary decision to marry Jack. Now he courts her out of pride rather than any feelings of love.

The above are the first steps in character development. We have clearly marked out the traits of our central cast. Their intentions, beliefs, and interrelationships are pretty much well defined. They haven't changed a whit . . . not yet. But with the arrest of Jack and his interrogation we give all our characters a chance at movement out of the ruts that so many of us inhabit from our first breath to our last.

Jack is certainly a coward. He's also a weasel of sorts. On the first day of his imprisonment he tells Dieter that he will seek an annulment if the charges are dropped. This forces the nationalist war-hawk to question his own motives. Jack's bald offer leaves nothing to the imagination. Dieter tells Jack that he will make him confess to espionage charges and see him on the gallows. Dieter tells his wife that the confession won't take more than the threat of pain to a man such as Morgul.

But Dieter is wrong. Working in character-contradistinction, Jack's cowardice will not allow him to confess, because confession is literally a death sentence. He undergoes horrendous torture but manages to keep the words *I am guilty* clenched between broken, bloody teeth. A coward with courage.

In the meanwhile, displaying great pluck, Ariel tells Bill that she will not abandon her husband because she sees marriage as a sacred institution as much as Bill sees war as destiny.

> "It doesn't matter that I don't love him or that we could literally have an annulment. I made an oath before God and country, and I will not break it. The charges against him are a joke. He does not deserve the treatment he's receiving."

The equestrian Bill, the war hero Bill, is not used to losing. On the farm he breaks horses. On the battlefield he breaks men. And he'll be damned if this woman's stubbornness will be any different. He beats her mercilessly, but she does not give in.

About the same time, Dieter realizes that Jack will never confess and that he has somehow failed himself by trying to make him do so. The screams from the victim are piteous and only make him seem that much more the hero. Dieter stops his inquisitor and visits awhile with the unconscious Jack.

Wracked by guilt, anger, and for the first time the sting of defeat, Bill decides the only thing to do is to eradicate the source of his pain—Jack. He goes to the prison and is admitted because he'd been there many times before. He has a gun and intends to use it . . .

The story, of course, does not end there. Does Bill kill Jack? Does Dieter kill Bill? Maybe they all die in the corridors of that dank, dark domain. Maybe Jack tries to break out. Maybe he succeeds. And what of Ariel?

The way I'd like for this story to end would be for Jack to be freed and for him to go to the hospital to visit Ariel. She is no longer classically beautiful, and he has been castrated. She asks him would he like an annulment, and he says that he'd rather they renew their vows.

My purpose in these character sections is to show, primarily by example, what character is capable of and how we might discover change in our characters. The story I put together here is more like a play than a novel, but there's little difference between the two when it comes to the emotional development of the protagonists. I'm also trying to show that the transmogrification of a person most often depends on interrelations. I suppose that a person could transform while working with and against events in nature. A hurt hawk or a rabid bear might force something to come to the surface. But in these cases the animal becomes the other side of the relationship. You might have someone alone in the desert or on Mars. But even here, I believe, different personalities would rise from the inner experience of the solitary character.

Whether you work up a bio on your characters before writing the novel or just jump in hoping to find their quirks and certainties while the story develops, you need the characters to grow or diminish and change, for better or worse. The world of fiction is always in flux, and its inhabitants are flotsam, seeking refuge in each other on the relentless tide of story.

Odds and Ends in the Character Bin

Whom do you believe?

Every story is a mystery of one sort or another. The reader might first be drawn in by something inexplicably beautiful or confusing, something that seems strange or maybe just slightly out of place. Interest might be piqued by a turn of phrase or a bald truth that is familiar. Sometimes the first words are bold enough that the reader wonders how the writing could prove its boast. But after a while the reader wonders only two things: 1) what happens next, and 2) what does it all mean: how will it turn out in the end?

A woman staggers out of the desert into a small town that doesn't remember her—at first. Who is she? What brings her here? What would cause her to make such a journey? Has there been some kind of accident? Why does she seem familiar to the crazy old man who lives at the edge of town near the junkyard? Why does she seem knowledgeable about the older parts of Lucasville, the places that were razed decades ago?

She could just answer these questions in a straightforward manner. Or maybe the memories were burned out of her head in the desert. Let's say she tells the sheriff that her car broke down two days ago on a hard dirt road that had little traffic—and no kind souls. A few pages later she tells the grocery-store clerk that her boyfriend, Brick Arnold, kicked her out of his car after an argument; she couldn't blame him though—after all, she had confessed to sleeping with his brother. Then a little boy with a toy gun sits next to her on a bench in a small park named after Robert Lucas, the founder of the town.

"That wasn't his real name," I told the boy.

"What was his name?" he asked me. He was enchanted the way only children can be.

I gave him a section of my orange and told him. "His real name was Bo Martin, and he came here because he killed a man named Jojo in East Saint Louis."

"What's your name?" the boy, called Soso, asked.

"Sandra," I said. "Sandra Filomene."

We know she's lying because she tells different stories to everyone she meets. She might well be called a *lying narrator* because no one, including the reader, can trust a word she says. The reader might soon tire of the tale because there's not one true thing that they can hold on to.

Then Brick Arnold arrives in town with a suitcase he says belongs to a woman named Filomene. The grocer warns her that Brick is around. The sheriff says that a Mr. Arnold left her property with him. Miss Lottie, the widow, offers to put Sandra up in a room at the back of her knitting-supplies store.

"I have a shotgun, Miss Filomene, and no brute will get through me."

As you can see, the mystery of the story is deeply intertwined with the fabrications of the woman calling herself Sandra Filomene. As we slowly come to understand the truths concealed beneath these lies, we will uncover the rotten heart and real history of Lucasville.

Or, using third person narration concentrated only on Sandra, we might have her coming out of the desert lying her butt off without the reader knowing it—at least not immediately or directly. She says that she is Sandra Filomene from East Saint Louis on her way to Phoenix to attend a friend's wedding. The car ran off the road and broke down, forcing her to leave all her belongings behind, hoping she had the strength to find someone to help her. Then Brick Arnold arrives, distraught that he put Sandra out of his car eighteen miles outside of town. This new wrinkle brings Sandra's story into question.

But our questions might just as well be about Brick. Maybe he's lying. Maybe he tried to rob or kill or rape Sandra—maybe all three. Maybe she also has a secret that keeps her from reporting the attack.

After going at the story from these differing perspectives, the author feels that it's too contrived and decides to craft a narrative voice that simply tells the story.

But after a few weeks on the straight-and-narrative path, the writer realizes that he didn't go far enough with the not-completely-trustworthy approach. He makes up his mind to split the narration between two minor characters who cannot be wholly believed for different reasons.

First, he turns to the crazy old man. He's called Mad Mackie by the townspeople. He lives in a tepee near the junkyard, has a coyote as a pet, and always seems drunk but has never been seen drinking or buying liquor.

Mack calls Sandra by the name Nelda and tells long tales about when she was the princess of Lucasville—a time long before her actual birth. Sandra brings Mack oranges and listens attentively to his stories about her. He warns the town elders that Sandra has come to pull down their dirty drawers and burn Town Hall, the oldest building in Lucasville, to ash.

Then the writer turns to the smitten boy, called Soso by his uncle and Jesse by his mom. Soso is in love with Sandra. She asks him to call her Nelly and says that she knew his absentee father and that his father loved him. The way she talks to the boy we don't know whether she's just trying to make him feel better or if maybe she knows more about him than we've been led to believe.

Soso talks about Nelly all the time. She gave him a bath and flew him to the moon. She told him that Mad Mackie's coyote was a girl and at night Mack turns into her coyote husband. And she told him that Robert Lucas was really Bo Martin who killed a man in a place called Louie and then he built Lucasville . . .

You may never use points of view like this in your fiction, keeping your secrets held in other ways. But it is worthwhile, I believe, to attempt to tell a story from its negative spaces, to allow the reader to wonder what is real before you reveal the truth, affording the reader an understanding of the lies told to keep the narrator safe and sound—she believes.

* * *

In spite of what we're told, truth is a rare commodity in the modern world. People lie all the time. On résumés, first dates, in their clothes, and to their children when they ask questions they don't believe they should know the answers to. We lie to strangers who need a helping hand and to our parents when they want to know what we did last night.

"It's not you, it's me," or, "No, there's nobody else." Are you straight or gay, man or woman, black or white or what?

I love you, a man says to a woman. She replies, I love you. He's telling his truth and she is telling hers. But what one hears may not be what the other means. As a matter of fact it probably doesn't mean the same thing. Often just that fact, that you love me, is enough. But sometimes, more often than we'd like to believe, that schism between what I say and what you understand can bring us into treacherous territory. Great for fiction, not so good for the characters therein.

Working with Character in a Hail of Words

Describing a human life—its passions, beliefs, scars, and successes—while having only the use of words is a daunting task. This difficulty is only increased when you realize that this is just the first step in a novel. Now you have to take this fully realized person and detail his or her journey and subsequent metamorphosis through the obstacle course of story. No photographs, recordings, musical accompaniment, props, or environments are available to help the reader—or writer. All either of you have is language and a smattering of punctuation.

Language. The word sounds like a root vegetable kept in a wooden crate on the winter porch. Soil-encrusted rutabaga or carrot, parsnip or leek. It sustains you but does not have the spark of a spring day or the solemnity of a hurricane. Regardless of these limitations, language is and always will be the New World. It contains our history and potential. Language condemns us or sets us free. The subterranean, subconscious warrens of our words contain and reveal us without our full knowledge.

Our job is to create a concrete world populated by unique, well-defined and yet shifting characters. The only tools we have are abstract words and the readers' varying abilities to make sense of them. This is a big topic. I'll come at it in a few ways in this monograph, but in the end you'll find that the subject is inexhaustible.

At this point, however, all we have to worry about are the words that describe and reveal the characters we are creating. To explore the use of words in fictional prose it is essential to consider two devices: 1) the narrative voice and 2) dialogue and his cousins.

Narrative Voice

You have some choices here.

1) You could use the first-person narrative voice; the I of the novel. This account of a story most commonly comes from a single character's point of view (POV) and is limited to the range and depth of that individual's predilections, prejudices, senses, experience, education, sophistication, immediate needs, age (maybe), and emotional responses.

2) There is the option of using second-person narration, which includes the reader as an actor in the fiction. This device works primarily by using the pronouns associated with *you*.

You walk into the room. You smell the wino's harsh breath. You wish you hadn't come.

I personally don't find second-person useful in fiction, because knowledge can be better contained within the book. Second person has more purchase in songs and poems—and how-to writing, like portions of the monograph you're reading now.

3) Then comes the most used form—the third person narrative. I like to think of this narrator as a voice perched on the shoulder of one or more characters in the book.

Joe saw Morley coming. He nearly turned to walk away but then their eyes met. He gritted his teeth, forced a smile, and said, "Hey, More, over here."

This narrator does not have full access to Joe's emotions and thoughts. But he does have at least a physical sympathy with the character, and this is enough to suggest the nature of Joe's emotional responses. The entire novel could be told through a third-person interpretation of Joe moving through his world. Or, when the conversation between Joe and Morley is over, the third-person narrator can jump to Morley's shoulder and follow him into the next phase of the story.

This ability to jump shoulders makes third-person narration extremely flexible. You aren't limited to one point of view but are admitted to as many characters' experiences as necessary to understand the world.

Third-person narration doesn't have the depth of knowledge of first person, but such limits might also be a benefit, giving the author the challenge of understanding people the way we do in everyday life.

4) The last category of narration is the universal (or omniscient) narrator, or—as you know her—God. And I'm not talking about some pantheonic Olympian deity here. I mean the Judeo-Christian One God. She knows everything throughout the universe. She can talk about three people sitting around a table lying to each other and then hop onto the back of a fly that takes her into an idyllic field where rotting corpses lie.

This is a potent voice, and you have to be absolutely certain about every word, every nuance and assertion. There are no maybes or *possiblies* in the universal narrator's voice. The people she talks about can be uncertain—but not her.

Using the universal narrator's voice is like drinking a tumbler full of heavy cream—a little too rich for most people's palates.

Lots of choices. And even more when you consider that, to some degree, you can blend narrative
forms. Maybe you have a preface told in a universal
voice to start a novel, the rest of which is related in
the first-person mode. Maybe your third-person narrator has a deeper, almost first-person, understanding
of one character but a less intimate comprehension
of others.

Lots of choices, but they all hinge on one important question: What is the best POV for the story you're
telling? For the most part this decision is based on common sense. For instance, if the story is about your main
character, and that character is interesting, engaging,
and articulate, then you may want to go straight to first
person.

If the breadth of the story covers many places,
classes of people, and levels of expertise, then some
form of third-person narration is probably preferable.
But there are other reasons one may choose third person. You might, for example, have an angry main character who is well spoken but does not have access to
deep self-reflection. You plan to spend every moment
with this guy, but having him speak to the reader won't
reveal much.

You may have a few engaging, intelligent, and expressive characters. In this case you might break the

novel up into sections or chapters given to different individuals to relate in the first-person voice. All I'm saying here is that you have to decide on the point of view or views of the tale. This decision might come before you start writing or as you become better acquainted with the story by writing it.

The narrative voice is temporarily suspended in fiction when an external declaration or image intervenes to disseminate information. This device might be a road sign that reads, DEAD END EXCEPT FOR BEAVERTON. It could be a loudspeaker declaring, "All girl children under the age of thirteen are to report to the blue hut, immediately." I once walked into a store and when I broke the laser eye, instead of the gentle two-tone beep I was used to, a recorded voice said, "Hey, sailor."

There are all kinds of potential voices, signs, and even images that don't adhere to the narrative voice(s) used to tell your tale. A character might be reading a book or being read to. He might peek over someone's shoulder at a newspaper. The sparing employment of devices such as these can add greatly to the storytelling, giving the reader another way to be admitted into the experience of that world.

* * *

There is one other external voice that eschews the limits imposed on the narrator—that is dialogue.

Characters speaking have the ability to break the rules narration must try to adhere to. For instance: you might have a sophisticated and genteel first-person narrator who spends his time ministering to the needy. He distributes food and rent chits, warm clothes, and toys for homeless children.

One day this man comes across a poor woman. He smiles at her.

"Who the fuck you lookin' at, motherfucker?" she responds.

Her words are a wonderful break in mood. They might even be used to bring out a new aspect of the nature of our courteous humanitarian. We discover that he really despises the poor, looks down on them. This woman doesn't give a damn about his soft hands and perfect teeth.

"You so slick you prob'ly ain't took a shit in five years," she comments.

This is one way to break up the mood, the language, and the voice of your story. But there are so many other ways that dialogue can help in the design of the world we're telling. You might need to explain an experience to the first-person narrator that he was not privy to. Maybe someone lies about, begs from, dismisses, or in some other way attempts to negate the dominant voice of the book.

These tools are useful in bringing in differing POVs and also breaking the monotony that might set in when all the words, descriptions, and thoughts begin to sound the same.

Every word is important; every word. And every word is about your characters, the world they live in, and how that world transforms them while it transforms around them.

Physical Description
A Note on Details

Every word is important. This means you have to use the right words to tell the tale, and it also means that you must use these words frugally, parsimoniously. There are so many things happening at any given moment in any situation that it would take thousands of pages to describe the smallest of events in its totality.

Take, for instance, a catatonic paraplegic lying abed in an all-white hospital room. Sounds simple enough. I might have exhausted the description already. Except we may need to know the gender of the patient... and his or her age. How long has he or she been there? Does the length of stay show up in his or her grooming? What does it smell like in there, and who comes in to visit or minister to the lump of flesh? Is there a window? A fluorescent light fixture? Are there machines attached to the patient, either keeping him or her alive or reporting electronically that life yet remains? Do attendants, nurses, and doctors talk over the paralyzed, comatose victim? What do they say, write down, or otherwise busy themselves doing? Maybe they kiss each other or the patient. Maybe they steal the patient's drugs or personal belongings.

Does the patient have a name? Yes, Stillman. Is there a fly buzzing at the window, bumping against the glass seemingly at counterpoint with the constant beeps and gasps of the life-gauging machinery? Maybe it's a hornet, not a fly. What lies outside that window? What time of day is it? Is there a TV on a metal stalk tuned to a station that plays old sitcoms day and night? If so what show is playing? What ads have you selected for the reader to hear?

Is the door to the room open or closed?

The room is white, but is it tidy? If it's dirty, does someone come in to clean? Maybe there's a spider perched at the very top of the window. Every time the fly or hornet gets close, she hunches in expectation of a meal.

What are the dimensions of this chamber? What's the temperature setting? And, of course, what brought Stillman to this physical condition? What are Stillman's chances of at least regaining consciousness?

What do people feel about him? Is he a hated criminal who preyed upon the elderly? Was he a great leader who survived a train wreck? Maybe he loved a woman who was in a loveless marriage but the husband shot him on principle. This last notion could lead us to a story outside the sickroom, but this exercise is about only what is contained within.

Have we exhausted the room and its content, its permanent and transitory inhabitants? We haven't said whether there is a roommate or visitors' chairs, dust bunnies stuck to the underside of the mattress, or any decorations, but it seems as if we've detailed enough—except . . .

. . . there's just one more thing: Stillman's mind. For the hospital employee, attending doctor, and even for family and friends who come to visit, the contents of Stillman's mind are inaccessible. But we are writers. There's no place we can't go. We can't go everywhere but we can go anywhere. If the title on the dust jacket of our book says STILLMAN, then we might have to break current real-world conventions and enter the mind of the man so mistreated by my words here. And once that door has been opened there's no end of detail available to our keyboards and pens, pencils and voice recorders.

The door is open, but we won't go through. There's not enough time or space to say everything about Stillman's thoughts, process of thinking, awareness or lack of same. Really there's not enough time or space to completely describe the room and Stillman's condition therein. But even if there were, a novel is not a laundry list but a story with a purpose. It's about character and place and time and society and politics and . . . so much. Our job is to pare away the extraneous while accenting the essential without letting it seem that what we're presenting is anything other than the everyday, the pedestrian experience of life that leads now and then to the unexpected and extraordinary, the satanic and divine.

It would be a good exercise for any writer, all writers, to place themselves in what they deem a very simple setting and then try to make an exhaustive description of the environment. I expect that for most beginning writers, this would be an enlightening exercise. Describe your kitchen or the process of your responsibilities and activities during the first hour at work; this is to include a detailed description of your work area. Use your acumen and imagination to find and explore every element of the place or task. Approach this chore assiduously and you will experience the avalanche of detail involved in even the smallest part or position of your day.

After this (hopefully humbling) experience, let's take on a project you're more likely to encounter while writing your novel.

Instead of visiting a white and antiseptic hospital room containing an unconscious, unmoving male patient we go to Grand Central Station in Manhattan at rush hour. There we will encounter two men and a woman who are there for various reasons of their own but are destined to meet and interact for purposes, large and small, in the story we're telling. There are literally millions of details available to the writer. But in your twenty- to thirty-page chapter you will use no more than a few hundred of these, probably fewer.

Some of the details will be salient to the story. The characters for instance. The woman, Abigail, is lost. She needs directions. One of the men, Charles, is looking inappropriately at the sway of her hips, but she notices only that their eyes meet. She asks him for directions. He knows most of the answer but not one important detail. Another man, Filo, has been watching. He inserts himself into the conversation adding the needed information. Then all three head in the direction the woman needs to go.

That's where we want to be in this stampede of people and information. But if we went straight there, the story would be linear and lifeless. So maybe, using a shoulder-hopping third-person narrative voice, we follow each of our characters from just outside the station to the moment they all come together.

Charles has just lost his job, and not coincidentally, his girlfriend has sent him a text—ending their relationship. He buys a hot dog and talks to the vendor about the subway series, Yankees versus Mets. Abigail is just in from JFK Airport, has never been in New York before, and needs to board a train for a hamlet a little north of the city. She asks a few people for help before Charles, but their responses are either rude or dismissive. Filo enters the station. He goes to the center of the main hall and scans the thousands of faces moving about. It is only when he sees Abigail and Charles that he seems to find purpose.

When crafting this scene we want the reader to feel the hustle and bustle, the sounds and mirth, the distinctly human desires, and the workaday world: humanity in all its potential and decline. We want everything, but we need only snatches here and there: an elderly woman barely able to stagger through the crowd, a toddler boy who has eyes only for his mother, young and old lovers, cops, and maybe a pickpocket pretending to be having a conversation on a cellphone.

It may seem to be a challenge to set the above scene in a paragraph or two. You may think you'll need help figuring it all out—help or maybe twenty extra pages. But you have only a page or two to prepare for your characters. And you already have the best help any writer can ask for—the reader.

The reader is a willing participant in the creation of the world of your story. She's hungry for the mystery of the three characters, the clatter and music of life, the almost choreographed movement of bodies, and the innumerable bit players inhabiting this world. If we take our experiences and distill them for the reader, she will want to take us the rest of the way.

So, after setting the time and place and numbers in the crowd, we start, maybe, with a loudspeaker announcing the next train to Naugatuck. This blends in with the pickpocket talking gibberish into his cellphone. Abigail hears the nonsense, turns to see the man as he lifts another man's wallet . . .

That's all you'll need for the reader to fill in the scene with either experience or imagination. After all, in real life we remember only in snatches of detail and pluck memorable moments from a seemingly endless flow of events. Both Charles and Filo run different, but still ordinary gauntlets that will end by bringing them all together.

Once you have the trust of the reader, he will help you along as long as you keep the characters seeing and experiencing the world in ways that are mostly recognizable. I say *mostly*, because the story is going to be a rarefied experience. Charles, Filo, and Abigail might seem to be pretty normal people in a world we recognize, but as the story unfolds we might find that Filo is investigating Abigail. Maybe she stole something from his friend or client. Or possibly Abigail and Filo are running a scam on Charles. Maybe Filo only seems to be watching Abigail, but his sights are really set on Charles.

These character interactions might be somewhere beyond the experience of many readers. But because you have described a place and experience that they could inhabit with their imaginations, they're willing to go a step or two further. This is another of the primary pillars that bolster the house of fiction: create a pedestrian world with characters in familiar but interesting circumstances and you have the foundation for story and deep investigation.

Maybe Filo's client has lied to him. Maybe Abigail saw Charles looking at her butt. Maybe she's a geneticist, a scientist who has to make a serious philosophical decision about a discovery that she and her now-dead partner made. We might go places that the reader could never imagine, but he's willing to follow because we have paved the way with everyday, ordinary experience.

The everyday. The ordinary. It sounds so simple, but as we saw above, it takes a great deal of specificity and choice. We can't present the ten thousand souls passing through Grand Central Station in the background of our story. But we can't ignore them either. An aged woman, a cop, a pickpocket. The guy selling hot dogs has an understanding of human nature that is so deft, he asks Charles, "Was she worth it?"

Just enough for the reader to believe—not a syllable more.

And you have to remember: only the important, the salient, the revealing details should be used in describing any place, situation, person, or thing. These details can't seem so important when we read them, but they are the necessary building blocks of the world that the reader will have to believe in.

The open piano sitting like a croc waiting for its next meal. Martin's dead eye somehow expressing ecstasy. The oversize beer can that fit his fist like a shot glass. Small, pedestrian, poetic—it doesn't matter. Get in there and show us where we are, what we're facing—then get out and let the readers do their job.

You and the reader make the novel.

Description:
Odds and Ends
Emotional Description

Physical sensations can be among the most difficult experiences to describe. An itch for instance: in most cases just the word itch works well enough. Usually all we have to do is talk about intensity. Is it a mosquito bite or one of those unreachable, almost painful attacks that wrench you out of sleep and keep you tearing away at a distress that refuses to respond?

But what if you were speaking to someone who did not have certain tactile neuronal responses? This person has never felt an itch or a tickle. How could you explain, without boring technical jargon, what it's like to experience this physical phenomenon? In the physical sense, how would you explain the word *feeling* at all? Maybe this person does experience hunger, headache, exhaustion, and a dry tongue now and again. Maybe you could suggest that the pain of a headache might be winnowed down to a pinpoint existing just below the skin on your wrist. You say that it seems like, if you could just dig at that point with a fingernail, it would break off, taking the irritation with it. But when scratching it, the pain, the itch only gets worse.

Not a perfect description. But it might do. And, more, it could lead to a metaphorical entrée into the heart of the story you're telling—the discovery of an itch to a man who has never had to scratch.

But what if we were talking about that classic seven-year itch? What if we were trying to explain love? You could say that Joe loves Josephine or that Josephine no longer loves Joe. Both these statements could be true. But they are bland and without depth. We don't know what either Joe or Josephine feels, because love is like a mutant itch; it's different in every heart.

When you want to create the intensity of love (or hate or infatuation or nationalism) you can't just say that that's how the character feels. A character cannot say "I love you" without some corroboration in the surrounding prose.

For example:

Whenever Joe saw Josephine his hands began to quaver and his breath came up short. He would suddenly remember a chore that needed to be done and hurry off.

One day, when he saw Josephine standing in the hallway with Janine Murphy, Joe dropped his Styrofoam coffee cup and rushed up the stairs, mumbling something about needing to find a mop.

"Every time I see Mr. Cordon," Josephine says, "he seems to be running off."

"I think he likes you," young, redheaded Janine said, smiling with her teeth.

"Noooo," Josephine replied. "He doesn't even know me . . ." Then, with a suggestive, shrewd smile, she added, " . . . yet."

This is not love itself but the prelude to something that may never occur. Your reader not only needs to understand what the characters are feeling but also how those feelings manifest themselves. They need to see the ebb and flow and the play that precedes the kiss.

Maybe Josephine gets Joe to slow down long enough that they make a date. Shy Joe tells Josephine that he used to dream about having a job like this. When she asks how it feels now that it's real he tells her that he feels gratitude—that when he wakes up in the morning he has to slow himself down so as not to go in too early.

Josephine is moved by Joe's longing for who and what he is. She's drawn to his passion. And his passion is for her.

"It was like a force I couldn't resist," Josephine tells Janine at some point along the way. "Like I was looking into a mirror in some fairy tale, and it was drawing me into a world that held the magic I always wanted."

"Unicorns and everything, huh?" Janine says, and they both laugh hard.

In the throes of lovemaking, Josephine asks where Joe got that jagged scar on his back. He is so captivated by her beauty and her willingness to share that beauty with him that he confesses he'd been in prison for his unwilling part in a robbery twenty years before. The scar came from learning the hard way, the only way you can learn behind bars. He begs her not to tell their boss, because then they'd have to let him go.

The boss finds out. Joe is fired immediately, which takes from him the same magic that Josephine was drawn to. Now Joe hates Josephine. He calls her unrepeatable names, sends e-mails, texts, and letters labeling her a traitor and a whore.

Josephine's response to Joe's vituperation makes sense, even if we wish that she had not taken the path she chooses. She works hard to get back into a room with him. She uses his reverence for his mother to do so. Once they're together she explains that she wrote an answer to an e-mail he sent when they were both still infatuated. She had no idea that this e-mail address created an automatic CC to his boss's secretary.

They go to his apartment, make passionate love, and fall asleep. Tomorrow will be a better day.

But in the morning Joe finds a letter from Josephine saying that she does love him, but she sees that his ardent heart is flawed, that he could never forgive her if she really made some kind of mistake or actually did something wrong.

Unemployed and alone, Joe sits on his bed eating barbeque potato chips. He calls his best friend, Martin, back home in Cincinnati, and explains what happened pretty much accurately.

"Well," Martin says, "I can see what she means. You do have a bad temper with all your secrets and stuff."

"You're supposed to be on my side," Joe retorts.

"I am on your side, man. It's just that your side is wrong."

Where does the story go from here? I have no idea. I wouldn't want to be in either Joe's or Josephine's position. But I believe we have gone a long way toward expressing how love feels within and between these characters. We cannot save them, only see them.

All this has been to say that describing emotion needs to be tied to character and how that person manifests his or her heart—consciously and unconsciously. It's like real life—only deeper.

Description as Poetry

Poetry is the heart of all writing. Passion, detail, music, just the right word, a sense of play, and a sense of tragedy that take us beyond even the pale of death. Without poetry in our words, our songs, our love lives, life would become impossibly dull, calcified, and worthless.

In the body of this book I will only use the idea of poetry in its contribution to the task of description. Poets know how to describe things. They take on weightlessness and gravity, time and loss, and those ghosts that hover around us, playing out old routines from centuries before while we go through similar steps in the *real world* today.

The following is a poem by one of America's premier poets, James Wright.

Lying in a Hammock at William Duffy's Farm
in Pine Island, Minnesota

Over my head, I see the bronze butterfly,
Asleep on the black trunk,
blowing like a leaf in green shadow.

Down the ravine behind the empty house,
The cowbells follow one another
Into the distances of the afternoon.

To my right,
In a field of sunlight between two pines,
The droppings of last year's horses
Blaze up into golden stones.

I lean back, as the evening darkens and comes on.
A chicken hawk floats over, looking for home.
I have wasted my life.

This lovely verse (an echo of Rilke's *Archaic Torso of Apollo*) gives us a man's pedestrian idyll, with no feeling of the humdrum. Instead, it's a confession; a moment in that life where he sees the deep beauty that has surrounded him—always. The miracle of life had been going on while he was distracted. But now, as he rests, he experiences the seemingly unconnected moments that make up eternity. The cows attached to those brass bells, the butterfly, and the soaring chicken hawk are all in the same mortal predicament; they are, each and every one, involved in the sweet struggle to survive. And so there is beauty as well as sorrow in this moment of ecstatic revelation.

You need poetry in your life or your words will never sing with the divinity of the ordinary.

Describing an Idea

You can, more or less easily, explain the phenomenal world either inside your body or outside: heat, cold, pain, size, shape, color. The physical world comes with its own pair of crutches, as far as explanation is concerned. Most of us know what you're talking about when you say, "He stood about six foot high." We understand *red*. But "the ache of morning" will have different but specific meanings to many. Such words are ideas that are corroborated by the experience of what we call reality. Sometimes they're semiabstract physical concepts, like gravity. We understand because we have experienced gravity and seen it in action. Sometimes that physical sense becomes a metaphor, as when you say, "There was gravity to her words."

But I'm not talking about the simple push and pull associated with the manifestations of the material world. I'm talking about the roots of fiction—ideas.

* * *

A good deal of hard science is embodied by fiction before it becomes reality in the hands of physicists, machinists, researchers, and so forth. Jules Verne's submarine, the *Nautilus,* was a machine of wild speculation before it was realized in mechanical form. We create by imagining and it is the role of fiction to suppose and then engender.

The soft sciences are even more challenging for the fictionist to use in her works. Theories like the economic infrastructure, the unconscious, and evolution all vie for explanation of what's happening in the physical world, but they have not yet developed machines or physical techniques to prove themselves. Therefore their ideas and predictions are often very hard to prove, and maybe even harder to understand.

Let's say you've discovered a reality in your fictional world that says, if a man or woman does not understand, and have empathy for, the plight of people around them he or she will experience the same fate. This fact doesn't have to be true anywhere outside your novel. But in order to make it real you need to bring this philosophical sense into a physical, sensual experience; you have to make me see the character's blindness that, in the end, will condemn him.

One of your Iago-like main characters follows a child who might potentially cause him trouble later on. The beautiful boy is nervously leaning over a precipice, titillated by the fear and the awe-inspiring view. Your character runs up behind the child, scoops him up, and tosses him over the side. Before falling the child grabs the man's hand, looks him in the eye, and pleads, "Help!" The killer feels the desperate tug, is almost pulled along with the boy. But the child's grip breaks, and he screams as he falls and falls and finally is blasted into pieces upon hitting boulders below.

Because the boy grabs him, looks him in the eye, and pleads for help, the killer identifies with his victim, feels that this is also his end. What he'd done to the boy could also happen to him. It is but a moment's revelation, which he dismisses, saying to himself, "But I didn't die."

By allowing the killer a moment of insight we have created the germ of an idea that could very well define the entire novel. And even though we might not have much sympathy for the murderer, his revelation could also apply to the child's parents, playmates, and the queen of the land, who, in the end, cannot feel empathy and, because she never gets her hands dirty, has no opportunity to have that moment in which she can understand the consequences of ignorance.

This is an idea and it has been described in the experiences of your characters. It is at once intangible and also real enough to take a life.

Taking a Breather

Looking back over this monograph as it has progressed so far, I get the feeling of a kind of metaphysical tidal wave as it recedes from the scene of devastation. The detritus tossed up appears with no particular rhyme or reason, order or plan. This is because the novel that comes from the natural disaster of experience at first makes no more sense than the brutalized woman punished by a man himself brutalized by war, all inside of a life that at one time seemed to make sense.

There's not only human debris in the wake of our literary tsunami. There are political movements and hunched up arachnids, the evil that comes from ignorance and different kinds of love speeding toward each other at breakneck speed. Giant children splash in the waters out beyond the continental shelf. And the stuttering story seems to start over and over like little cousins of the great wave smoothing opaque stones that contain and conceal the essence of our tale.

There is no identifiable plan or plot to the partial descriptions and definitions of the structure of revelation as far as it pertains to the novels we wish to discover through our writing. There might be a sense to the stories, but they don't make sense in the way of scientific theorems or the letter of the law. Impossibly, the novel is an entire world squashed down to the size of a coconut. You can carry it in one hand, throw it against the wall, or place it next to you in bed so that when you wake up in the morning it awaits you like the hairy skull of some distant ancestor hoping for empathy.

That coconut is out there on the receding ocean, bobbing up and down. We're splashing around in a little dinghy looking for it, without knowing that we are—at least not exactly. There are other little boats out there too—other hapless mariners looking for who and what they've lost in this gallimaufry of wreckage, rubble, and debris.

Writing a novel will be that topsy-turvy, crazy-quilt journey, if you're lucky. It defies size, accessibility, and direction. It can be held in one hand, but at the same time it is as vast as any ocean. It is your culture and history, language and gender, hope for resolution and fate—and it is the opposite of all these things.

In trying to explain my understanding of what revelation is in relation to fiction, I hope to show that the first epiphany is for the writer to realize what she's been saying without knowing it. Once we see the truths unearthed by our attempt to tell a story, we open the door on character and also on the systems of a world informed by character, science, war, and the hankering for things that we now know we never really understood.

I suppose I'm saying that a novel is the ideal of flawed, floundering, and yet heroic humanity. Horny, hungry, happy, hard-pressed, hurt, and humiliated humanity. A woman who wakes up in the morning thinking once more about a mother who could not love her while at the same time listening to the song of a bright red bird sitting in the evergreen pine just outside the window. The novel is not in alphabetical order, the order of importance, or any other kind of systematized structure of content. It is pedestrian and divine. It is unexpected in its responses and yet perceived as fated in every word, phrase, character, and event. The novel is the epitome of mortality in a universe that seems to go on forever.

For these reasons I have approached this essay the way I would a novel. Explanations, examples, exhortations, and deep examination are all good and well, but I realize that I wanted the form of this document to reflect the *process* of novel writing; that floundering, flailing, frustrating fruit of the heart and mind where they come together—the intersection that defines the soul and maybe even the novel.

Voice(s) of a Novel

Let's continue with the idea that the novel, among other things, can be experienced as a living, breathing being, a more or less consistent, expressive being that has a modicum of intelligence and somewhat less knowledge than it needs. Because the novel is composed only of language, this living quality can be defined as Voice. That is—a sound and a vibration, an attitude and education, emotional limits and even character flaws that allow the reader to recognize and imbue that Voice with an identifiable personality. This is not a narrator but the actual quality of character created through the use of language. There might even be an opportunity to bond with the novel through empathy with this linguistic personality.

When you write a first-person narrative, the voice speaking through you is one solitary soul relating the tale as it is unfolding or as it has unfolded in the past (or in the future, depending). I like keeping this narrator as close as possible to the present for reasons that will become apparent.

This first-person narrator has a name. Let's call him Clem. He's from northern Minnesota and has a story about going to California to find his daughter, Elisa. Elisa's friend, Brook Gentry, traveled to Venice Beach with the young woman and has come back in pretty bad shape. She tells Clem that his daughter has fallen in with some shady people and needs saving.

Clem fires up his old Studebaker that evening and heads for the state known for its dreams and its disasters.

"The night was so beautiful," Clem tells us. "It made me think about Elisa when she was a child. We'd go camping alone together because her mother was too sensitive to bug bites. Elisa would make up stories about the stars until she'd fall asleep . . ."

We're right there with him, traveling through the northern forest, thinking about a child who is and was loved. Later on we will remain as close to the present moment of the novel as possible. Why? Because, as we've said, the novel is a journey of character, the roadmap of the emotional transition he and/or she will experience. The closer we can stay to the action of the novel the more clearly and intensely we will feel these changes.

There's no telling where Clem's classic Studebaker will take us. Maybe he'll pick up a young woman hitchhiker, Renee. This action is uncharacteristic for Clem, but because of his fears about Elisa, he doesn't want to think he left some other father's child by the side of the road where she might come to harm.

Maybe he'll break down or his car will. Renee's voice will be added to the choir that makes up the unique music, the Voice, whose chant and lingo become the unconscious Chorus of the novel.

Even in a first-person narrative there are many voices. Once you start adding characters there begins the contrapuntal intonation and litany of the tale. This musical back and forth, harmony or disharmony, creates the contours of the character of the novel, as Clem speaks, hears the words of others, and experiences signs, symbols, and sounds that appear via his narration.

Sooner or later Elisa will be found. The daughter of Clem's reveries is not the young woman he encounters. This new Elisa is wild, brash, and sensual in a way that scares her father. She rejects Clem, has her new cult friends beat him. The only reason he survives is Renee, who has moved into another kind of communal-living situation. She nurses poor Clem back to health and tells him, in a Voice as strong as the first-person narrator's, that he needs to let go and return home, to wait there until Elisa is ready to hear him.

Clem takes Renee's advice. He hates Elisa and the night sky and even the idea of loving somebody. Now the only thing he loves is his Studebaker. He tells us all this while driving back toward home.

He doesn't make it. The Studebaker breaks down not far from Death Valley, and he, while working to make enough money to fix his engine, gets a call from Renee. Elisa has gotten in touch with her. She's been punished by the cult in such a way that she now understands what she did to Clem.

While waiting for Renee to bring Elisa to him, Clem experiences an aria of character transitions. This near-hallucinogenic section of language reaches beyond Clem's conscious mind into the Voice of the novel. He remembers all that's happened to him, but in different ways. He imagines that Elisa is hatching a plot against him and plans to hurt him further. He decides that she is a devil-child and that he will have to kill her. His song, his voice has brought us from love to treachery to murder—and it isn't over yet.

Clem's character, along with those of Elisa and Renee and maybe others, transforms due to the story, the plot, even the plight (the context) of our working-class cast. Clem's voice, though it might sing different tunes, mostly retains this man's passions and loves, his strong beliefs, and his equally powerful confusion. We recognize the honesty in Clem's voice, and that allows us to slip deeper and deeper into the heart of the novel. Once inside we are addressed by another, whispering Voice. This is the tone and mood, natural genius and ignorance of a worldview, creating an aesthetic that is the underlying possibility for the truth that your manuscript is straining toward. Clem's story strikes a vein of either red blood or gold ore. He's telling the story. He may think the story is about his experience. But in reality the tale is beyond his ken.

The Voice that arises from the third-person narrative is that much more complex. Instead of one dominant POV, your novel could have many. Not one of these has the sustained POV of a first person. Third person is just that—a story told by someone outside the center of the tale as it unfolds. Because this narrator is not directly vulnerable to the events as they transpire, it cannot have as deep a connection. As a matter of fact, I have read and been told that the third-person narrator is an *objective* voice. I can understand the desire for this restriction. Once you allow the third-person narrator to have an opinion the exhibition of emotion makes that voice, to one degree or another, unreliable.

I understand trying to keep your third-person narrator unopinionated; that way, from shoulder to shoulder we can rely on the honesty of interpretation.

I understand, but at the same time I know that a human being writing anything has an opinion, regardless of the rules. The trick is to modulate the narrative voice so that it doesn't conflict with characters that speak and experience the story. For instance: toward the beginning of this section I said that Clem was headed for California, *the state known for its dreams and its disasters.* That is not an objective bit of narration. It is an opinion and a choice of a Voice that is a bit wry and also wants to warn the reader that there's danger up ahead.

This is a milder Voice than that of any narrator, but if it is managed it will be something the reader can rely on, possibly be surprised by, and hopefully something, someone that calls the reader back, again and again, to continue the journey to its ultimate end.

Voice is a subtle and yet indispensable part of any story. The tale is being related by one or more speakers. These speakers come together, creating a unique piece of music that sticks in the reader's mind's ear like the refrain of a popular song or, maybe, it sits by the reader's bedside—the assuring company of an old friend. It's something you can rely on whether you know it or not.

Rewriting

Do you ever find yourself going over a recent conversation, recalling every word said? Maybe it was a first date, and you spent most of the time babbling about yourself. You were being interviewed for a job and said something about the guy's nose. His nose? What's wrong with you? Or, conversely, a random individual insults your home state and it isn't until the next morning that you think of the perfect retort.

Words are continually spilling out of us or going unsaid when they're called for. We stutter, misspeak, tell the truth when we oughtn't, and often we say things that were true at the time but are no longer so.

The great range and flexibility of language not only allows for sublime expression but also makes room for error and vulnerability. Therefore every conversation is a potential minefield of its own making.

Wouldn't it be great to go back to that date and ask the right questions? Shouldn't you have told that guy with the big nose about your deep experience in communications? When BB kissed your neck at just the right moment, maybe *I love you* was not the appropriate response.

The truth is, you can't go back.

Move on. Let it go. Forget it. You cannot change what was or wasn't said. You can't make yourself into the better person of your intentions. The beauty of life is in its flaws and how you deal with them.

The beauty of writing is that you *can* go back and make the changes that will be everything you meant to say and not one word you didn't.

Writing *is* rewriting. The first draft is the jabber you forced on that blind date. She was hoping for someone to ask her what she was feeling, but all you said was, *and then I, and then I, and then I, and then* . . . The first draft is meant to be discarded. The first draft is the beginning of the idea, the slender thread of a story. The second draft is little better, as is the third, and the fourth and fifth. Writing is rewriting—a lot of rewriting. You think you know what you should have said on that job interview, but in truth it might have been a mistake even to go after that job. You said the wrong things on the date, but if you had said what you thought of the next day the ensuing relationship would have been a fiasco. You know it. You do.

The story isn't about perfection, at least not the glib perfection of just the right words or silences. The story is a living, breathing creature that often basks in awkwardness. The story is about not getting the girl, the job, the adulation of your parents' friends. The story, once you find it, encompasses an extraordinarily pedestrian, inarticulate, inappropriate world where the wrong words say the right thing.

> "How do you feel about me?" the young man asks on that first date you remember so well.
> "I . . . I don't know," she responds and then looks away.

It's the wrong question and a reply that is no answer. This snippet of dialogue, maybe twelve drafts into your book, accurately portrays the person at the top of this section, the hapless young man poring over the words he might have said. Writing is rewriting, and rewriting will bring you home.

Most of us understand the desire to be clear and articulate, respected and maybe adored. Fiction reveals to us how impossible and irrelevant these desires are. Our characters are searching for equilibrium in a little dinghy in the aftermath of that metaphysical tsunami. They are looking for meaning that resonates with their desire to understand. Words are the major tools for survival in the human realm.

The beauty of life is in its flaws and how you deal with them. The beauty of writing is how you deal with those flaws in character and plot, story and Voice, a novel that in the end understands and accepts unavoidable failure. Failure is how we learn. Failure tells us what's wrong. Failure is the only reason we have to get up again, and with it we gain the understanding and pain of misstep.

Rewriting is the way we address and reform ourselves, our language. You have to love this process, give in to it. Do not shirk. Do not say, *I've done enough,* when you know you haven't. Do not look for a bright future or happiness where there is none.

The novel is like Dorian Gray's portrait. It starts out beautiful, innocent, and hopeful. But as time passes, and we commit the sins of fiction, the portrait devolves under the decay and putrefaction associated with the hard labor of the writer rewriting the tale and discovering the reality that lies beneath. Absorbing our sins and failures, it loses perfection and instead is imbued with the rot and the stink of truth.

And one other thing. New writers often ask me, "Mr. Mosley, how do you know when a novel is finished?" My rote answer is couched in the idea of rewriting.

I say that once I finish a draft, I reread the book. There I find things that are wrong or that don't work. At that point I make the necessary changes through a new draft. I read the book again. More problems and another rewrite. This process might be repeated twenty times, more. Finally, I reread a batch of changes, see problems in the work, and yet realize that I have no answers. That is when the book is finished.

The novel will never be perfect and neither will you.

What's New?

Improvisation is an important element in the construction of any novel. You *are* making up a good deal of the story and its environs. In this way novel writing is closer to jazz than it is to the mathematical precision of the modern interpretation of European classical music. Don't get me wrong: Beethoven, I hear, could extemporize on his piano all night long, and it is said that many musicians of old Europe could think with their instruments. It's just that the music passed down to us has been codified and, to a certain degree, deified and defined. Through this process the art has lost some of its down-to-earth creative edge.

What does this attention to musical composition have to do with our novels? Everything. Most people know more than they think they do. Those same folks believe they know things that they do not. This odd anti-balance of knowledge and ignorance is clear in the construction of a novel. We write characters, they come from our minds, and yet they are not us—not at all. A successful character, Huckleberry Finn for instance, virtually steps off the page and into the minds and hearts of millions, maybe billions of readers down through the generations. We know more about King Lear than we do about Shakespeare. The *truths* about these fictional characters were made up—they had to be. They were created from the knowledge and passions, fear and loathing of individuals who simultaneously know and do not know what they're talking about. This, among other things, is the heart of improvisation.

Let us say there's a young black woman named Nora Lane. She's one of a few central characters in a legal thriller a novelist is writing that concerns sexual misconduct, in its many forms, in the justice system of Chicago. Nora has recently passed the bar and is assisting the major players in a far-reaching lawsuit. She's been brought in from Pittsburgh and is staying in a sublet on the South Side.

Every day Nora walks six blocks to a downtown train. This is her ritual. Nora is a very serious, even an obsessive, creature of habit. This makes her an excellent research assistant because she is methodical, concentrating on each detail of the job at hand without prejudice or passion.

One morning the novelist wakes up and reads about a shootout in Chicago. This gun battle is in Nora's neighborhood. The writer wonders what would happen to a creature of habit like Nora if she had to take a detour . . .

This is something new; something that doesn't follow the tight plotline the writer has envisioned. Because of the police action, Nora is forced to take a left where she usually walks straight ahead. This brings her through a rougher neighborhood than she's used to. She gets catcalls and a man or two tries to block her progress in order to get her attention. She decides she'll take Uber from now on. But then something happens.

A young girl, maybe fourteen, is sitting on a stoop crying her heart out. The adolescent is distraught, inconsolable. Nora stops, oddly fascinated by this spectacle of desolation.

An older woman comes to the girl's side and wraps her in her arms. The child wails and answers a few questions that Nora does not hear. The older woman shouts to Nora to come over and help. Nora approaches tentatively. The woman says that it was this girl's brother who was slaughtered up the street.

"Her older brother?"
"No."

They help Angelique, the child, to a room that she and her twelve-year-old brother rent from a Peruvian family on the seventh floor. Angelique's brother, Bernard, known as B-Bear, was who and what she lived for. He looked to her for safety, and she's failed him . . .

We can stop the improv here for a moment. The writer never intended to bring a shooting, a victim, the sister of the victim, and a self-appointed social worker of the neighborhood into the tale. Nora, who was at first meant to be a quirky and yet enlightened love interest, has now become a wild card, who might see something beyond her rigid obsessiveness and education.

Again, the story we're writing is a living thing and has opinions of its own. As the writer, we are part of these decisions, but that doesn't give us, or our conscious minds, complete control.

Improvising with the very real characters we've created allows differing points of view to enter the tale. It admits the shootout and the fallout from that shooting, the story we want to tell, and another story that wants to be told. We have to remember that a novel attempting to rise above the level of mere story does not get there because of our knowledge and certainty, our education and intelligence alone. The novel flourishes when its author begins to take risks.

Throwing a shootout, gang warfare, and police indifference into the path of a main character will make her journey (and your rewriting) much more difficult. But it also allows Nora to wonder about the real victims of sexism—the children.

At first this schism calls for a major detour away from the slick and dangerous case in court. But Nora finds meaning in the long way home. She understands what the writer didn't know she was saying.

It's like magic, the relationship between the writer and the writing, the rewriting and the *real* world that impinges upon it. Intelligence, education, sophistication, and the craft of writing all potentially hinder a novel that is trying to be born. The story isn't there to expose the writer's brilliance or her intricate interpretations. It, the novel, is there to drain her lifeblood, to challenge her morals, and say that there exists a more vital life than her own.

To that end, when the Voice of the novel asks, *Why not take this detour and see if we can get something out of it?*—you should listen.

Nora is twenty-four. Her potential love interest, Sterling, is thirty-two. He is one of the principals on the team. Sterling is a Native American fellow, Hopi actually. He's so smart it hurts. Free ride through Harvard to Oxford and then back, finishing in law at Yale.

He takes a limo to work every morning.

But on a Wednesday, eight days after Nora has had her eyes opened to a different interpretation of the same old shit, Sterling's Tesla limo short-circuits and stops in the middle of a busy intersection. It's a nice enough neighborhood, and so he decides to take the train.

A young hip-hop busker, Adjoran, boards at some point, dropping rhymes about the morning commute of a man like him and most of the rest of the people on the train. Liberal Sterling gives him a generous donation.

Nora's work begins to suffer. She's representing Angelique in court, making waves for the cops who aren't investigating B-Bear's murder, and she's moved in with the social worker.

Becoming careless, Sterling gets on the train a little late one evening and is confronted by muggers who want to hurt him. Adjoran steps in and stops the beating but fails to save Sterling's money and jewelry. Sterling suspects that Adjoran was part of the mugging, but he doesn't tell the police this.

The next day Sterling takes the train and sees Adjoran. The lawyer says he knows the young man was part of the mugging. Adjoran smiles and says he can tell that Sterling went to one of those fancy schools, so he has a rhyme just for him. He does a beautiful Latin and English rap that contrasts and compares the two men. The name Adjoran comes from the Latin *hadria,* which means darkness: blackness on blackness is all he sees.

Of course, Adjoran has a backstory. But what's important is that Sterling, for the first time, begins to understand his self-hatred. He hides Nora's activities and, after a while, he begins to help her.

Adjoran, after hearing what Nora and Sterling do, says, "Like mowing the grass at the graveyard. It sure is pretty."

We may know the truth about the story we're telling but, given a little freedom on the leash, the story, if it comes from our heart, knows more.

Improv after the Improv

The section above talks about a detour, a forced improvisation that has a powerful and direct impact on the character and subsequently the story told. The journey taken by Nora brings her into a world that speaks to the court case she and Sterling are working on. Even though we might not see this connection at first, it comes clear as Nora follows and allows herself to become involved. As far as the structure of revelation is concerned, this deviation brings all of our characters into closer alignment with the tale we're telling, because the sexism intertwined with the racism piled on Angelique and her dependent brother makes them among the most vulnerable of Chicago's denizens.

The writer has been influenced by Nora's rigid characteristics combined with a news report. This added level of complexity reconceives a tale that might have otherwise become didactic. And yet, ironically, B-Bear's murder and Nora's left turn expose even more

the preachiness of the story, showing us that this improvisation also gets mired in sanctimony; it becomes
another nail in the coffin of institutionalized sexism.
And even though this is our goal, it has to be remembered that we're still writing a novel, which needs to be
governed by a different set of rules. We find ourselves
asking, what if Nora had turned right instead of left?

What if a man confronts her who seems to have
knowledge about her? He doesn't really, but emotion-
ally, maybe unconsciously, she's looking for something
that makes her believe he does. Maybe this guy thinks
Nora and her cohorts are trying to emasculate men. He
would make a good counterpoint to the story, but still we
are stuck in an idea that finds it hard to transcend itself.

Two improvs, and we have learned that our restless-
ness with the story is pressing against our own inelastic
commitment to the underlying arguments. Why write
a novel if there's nothing to learn? Why write a novel
if the only goal is to inform, instruct, and explain? You
believe in the politics of this story the way a farmer
believes in the spring. But what does that farmer think
when she looks out over the distance and sees a mile-
wide tornado bearing down on her farm?

That is the right question.

A killer storm has descended on us like some
demon sent to destroy our better selves, our hopes

and beliefs. That's the mood of the novel. Add to that heavy atmosphere Nora's rigid characteristics, which are quirks not character, and you have the potential for a deep dive into the humanity that lies beneath the surface, the touchpoint of the storm and the earth.

So . . .

Nora is stopped on her daily walk because of a police action up ahead. In her left hand she has her morning latte in a paper cup. Her briefcase handle is snugly clutched in the other hand. She's been thinking systematically about the research she's done and has yet to do. Her breathing is steady, dependable. Her boyfriend, Tibor, will call her from Pittsburgh at noon his time, eleven hers. There's an imposed balance on everything, everything.

"You have to go around, Miss," a police officer says. "There's been a shooting on this block."

Nora looks up at the woman and winces, feeling a pain that is not physical.

"You'll have to go around," the cop repeats.

Nora looks down the block to her left. It seems to go on forever and ever.

"Miss," the cop insists.

When Nora turns left her thoughts jumble.

Her left foot feels slightly heavier than the right, and the sun sits at an angle that bothers her eyes. After a very long block of this discomfort she decides to throw her latte away, but in her confused state, she tosses the briefcase into the public trash bin instead.

Two blocks later she sits on a bus stop bench and starts to cry. A man asks her what the problem is.

"Nothing," she says, a mind removed from the remorse of her body.

An older woman stops and asks the same question.

"Everything is lost," Nora laments.

I'm not sure where Nora's tale might go from here. It will be part of the story because it is part of the story. A novel is about people and their ability to change as much as it is about ideas. Novels aren't flowcharts or blueprints, GPS directions or faraway stars pointing the way west. Nora's breakdown is her mind's and body's response to a world gone out of control. That world is the chemistry of the blood and the alchemy of the mind.

This mental breakdown, this anguish gives us a touchstone in Nora's heart. Her throwing away the briefcase probably adds to the plot of the story. Her fellow workers' responses to her will reveal much about their parts in a world they're so sanctimonious about, happily becoming a way for the novelist to criticize herself.

Nora's story stands alone, but even while she loses the thread of the legal thriller, her part in this world remains.

This last notion is what's so important in our ability to shift away from the point we're so consciously trying to make. Drama is an interwoven tapestry in life as well as fiction. Good and evil, right and wrong blend into shades of gray and violet, orange and green. Love of life and the celebration of difference bring us to that moment of transcendence. There is no rule book for love. Human nature rules us just like that tidal wave, a last breath, and the many, many hungers that press us forward—or back.

You feel the need to break through the very good intentions that have begun to strangle your novel. Improvisation is a good way to achieve this end. And when you turn to this acting device it would be good to remember to employ the ordinary, the everyday, the pedestrian.

For instance, a mouse loose in the house. It can be heard burrowing in the walls late in the evening. An ache in the left knee. The memory of a strain of music that refuses to give up a title.

Your starting point could be a news item or an old saying your mother constantly misquotes. But it could also be something a little less dull. The doctor might have diagnosed cancer—in you or maybe an old mentor or friend. This is pedestrian inasmuch as it happens thousands of times every day.

Just because the departure point of the improv is somewhat unproductive at first doesn't mean the decision is a misstep. Maybe the writer hasn't gone far enough. Maybe this road frightens the writer, and so she doesn't go in with full commitment. What if the main character's mother or sister or daughter receives the dire diagnosis just when our heroine is crossing a professional threshold she's been approaching for a lifetime?

Echoes and Traces

Rereading this monograph I see how one unspoken theme has crept in without my awareness. That is, positing a bedrock element in writing fiction and then adding a slight echo that gives that element subtler and yet, hopefully, deeper tones.

For instance: we discussed narrative voice in some detail. The foundation of a novel is the voice or voices used to narrate the tale. That being said, I later spoke about the *other* Voice of a novel, this Voice being a faint echo that attends to environment, attitude, mood, place, and a particular (even peculiar) sense of the world.

To anchor character development, and to help on the journey, I used the example of character interaction. These connections, if properly employed, can showcase the changes of the heart without overtly telling us what those changes are. When referring to the blank page we came upon the notion that the blankness is only there because of the glut of knowledge, hopes, and intentions in the writer's mind. This brought us to the juxtaposition of the fearful mature writer and the bold child artist within.

And when speaking of the writer's mind, I had to pay homage to the truth that the novel is, has to be, larger than the capacity consciousness has to contain it.

The consciousness of the novelist is at times unbearable. He or she becomes stuck on an idea and in doing so loses the playfulness, the true drama, the humanity of the work. The novel has slowly turned into a treatise on gender interaction or the history of Hawaii—something wrought purely of thought, ideas, and ideals. The writing has taken on a religious tenor that believes in the truths it espouses before the characters can speak or even think them.

The novel is bigger than the writer's head. It is a mountain and she is an ant. It is a globular planet when he at first thought it was a vast flat plain. A novel is a realm of discovery, a place where the characters and the writer and the evening news come together to create something they had not, they could not, have known beforehand.

In order to address these problems, we used dramatic improvisational tools to kick-start characters into thinking, acting, and reacting differently. Sometimes this works and sometimes not. Even if an approach does not fix the problem, that doesn't mean it hasn't revealed part of the answer. Nora turned left—it didn't work. What if she turns right? That doesn't quite fit the bill either. But we have learned that our protagonist has to go somewhere. After a while of pondering it comes clear that this movement might not be physical; maybe it's internal, maybe it's her mind. Her sanity is as much in question as is the unhinged system of justice that has failed everyone.

A change like this is dynamic. The writer grabs hold of the story shifting the world, implementing power like Moses did with the Red Sea. The reader sees these changes clearly and either goes with them or not.

The value of this dynamic approach to the novel is clear. You need a change and you make one. The problem is keeping the conscious desires of the writer out. That is to say improvisation is potentially a good tool but it can be ham-fisted.

Another approach we might take is to implement a scientific term to turn down the volume on changes we use to expand the reach of our tale. The term is *trace element*. In the physical sciences these are chemical elements present in only minute amounts in a particular environment. These traces are essential to the health and maintenance of an organism or atmosphere. They have to be there but are, on the whole, invisible.

Fiction is not a science experiment, but there are hints and smidgens throughout a good novel that make the story a deeper, more powerful and entertaining form. Advice from a madwoman to a child, if properly formed, might instill sympathy in the reader. This reader will want to know more because of the dissonance and truth the madwoman brings into the life of a little girl. This interaction might not have a concrete connection to the story, but without it the lights inexplicably dim. These few lines of conversation might set off a vibration that, unexpectedly, comes up off the page and into the hearts of your audience, bringing the rest of the novel along with it.

These literary trace elements can take many forms: the weather, music playing on the other side of a wall, a fly that seems to live for weeks. A trace element could be the effects of a neighbor's diet over a dramatic period in another character's life or a quixotic clock that never quite tells the right time.

So let us say that Nora, in her unstable mental state, leaves the window to her little sitting room open on a hot, un-air-conditioned Chicago summer night. The next morning she's dreaming about her mother. She's had this dream before. It's sad and always ends in loss. Then there's a sound just as sad as the dream coming from the kitchen/sitting-room area.

A slightly wounded mourning dove has come in through the window. When Nora gets to the room she sees an alley cat on the fire escape ready to come in. She shoos the cat away, then sees that the bird is eating the seeds off a sesame-seed roll in the trash. Nora puts up the screen, places another roll on the breakfast table, and leaves the bird—all of this without much forethought.

This is not an ornithological treatise on plumage, beaks, and city dwellers other than human beings. Shelly, the female dove, and later her mate, Proud Peter, are there to reveal parts of Nora that the rest of the fiction will not, cannot show us. Maybe the birds will help in her revival from the mental breakdown; maybe not. It doesn't matter because a novel is not a single story with an exclusive end. There are many stories and directions and loose ends to the saga. The novel is deep and the writer is limited. The characters are ornery, uncommunicative, and ignorant, making the writer into a locksmith with his good hand tied back and the untrustworthy clock ticking on the wall.

* * *

There are even subtler traces. Colors and tints, light and dark, the sound of prayer and the evidence of infinity. Maybe an extremely loud el train passes by every time just before Nora can complete a thought. Outside the window are rows of short, squat houses and the glass skyscrapers they're reflected in. A solitary bird looking for home. These elements, these faint signs can be as important as any dramatic discourse you can fashion.

Open the window, then go take a nap. Wake up to the world of your novel, not the story you're telling. There's a big world of bugs and doves, news reports and detours. Your novel is embedded in this world and in the minds of every reader. Your improvisations and trace elements, that song you just remembered and the feel of grit between your toes—all of this is potentially necessary for the world you create, the world that's creating you.

Taking a Breather, No. 2

As writers in today's world, we are faced with all kinds of expectations that have nothing to do with our craft. These requisites arise from readers' and publishers' desire for specialization, the economics of book sales, politics of all stripes, and the political and economic goals of institutions of higher learning.

Someone asks, what do you do? You say, I'm a writer. That's a simple enough answer: I'm a bricklayer, an accountant, a nurse, a cook. Writer is a similar thing. But no. They ask, do I know who you are? What kind of writer? Screenplays, mysteries, poetry? Are you published? By whom? Is that how you make your money? Can I get your books anywhere? Are you any good?

A woman asked me the other day, "Are your books R-rated?"

I'd like to hear somebody ask a bricklayer if they're any good; probably get a Krazy Kat brick upside the head.

But for all these questions few people want to read your writing, not if they haven't heard your name. And, even if they do know who you are, they'd rather talk... and talk and talk.

You must read a lot, is often said. It's not actually a question but more a bland truth like commenting on the weather. I always tell people that reading is an important part of the modern world. The act of rereading forges the mind. But reading and writing, I go on to say, don't have a whole helluva lot to do with each other. After all, one of the fathers of the Western tradition of the novel is Homer, and he was both illiterate and blind.

If you write screenplays, people are more willing to give you a pass, thinking that if they're lucky they might get an intro to a movie star. Anyway, everyone believes they know what screenplays are because they watch so much TV.

Novelists and poets don't get off so easy. Where'd you go to school? I'm often asked. But let me ask, since when did universities and colleges hold sway over the contemporary written word? How many of the great writers of history were educated beyond the age of twelve? Some guy will read your book and then say, it doesn't quite hold up to Gide. Really? Here is this guy, who has read your book and found it lacking, according to some other guy, named Gide—whoever that is.

Universities and colleges have always produced snobs who feel that they know better because they've studied the best. But historically college was not the place one went to become a writer. In the last hundred years more and more writers have had some college in them, but most schools did not offer degrees in creative writing. Wisely, they sought to teach about what had been written.

Today our profit-hungry universities have discovered the gold mine of BFA and MFA degrees in creative writing. Twenty, thirty, forty, eighty thousand dollars a year to attend workshops with professional writers who may have had some modicum of success in the marketplace. I don't know of any such program that demands the instructors know how to teach.

These uneducated educators talk about Shakespeare and T. S. Eliot, George Eliot and Toni Morrison. They read your manuscripts because they've been paid to do so. They suffer students' arrogance because they're paid for that too.

This expectation, this offer of employment for writers seems at first to be a great boon to our poets and novelists, biographers and short-story masters.

"Have you heard of Tobias Major?" the dean of the English department asks a Wall Street alumnus.

"Didn't he win the Pulitzer a few years back?"

"We have him on the faculty."

We have him—teaching classes, attending faculty meetings, correcting papers, sitting next to you at dinners with other alumni who are wealthy enough to get invited. We have him . . . by the balls. We writers are expected to keep publishing companies afloat and then to fill the coffers of prestigious schools. Imagine it. There you stand, instead of writing, teaching a dozen students, each of whom is paying $8,000 to sit before you in that antiseptic classroom. That's $96,000 per class, and they pay most teachers maybe $15,000: $81,000 profit per class, for the school and the muckety-muck prizewinner they used as bait to bring in the young, soon to be deeply in debt, students who hope for the brilliant life of writing.

Universities don't make good writers, not any more than war, poverty, chemical imbalance, a good sense of humor, or a parent who loved it when you told stories. I know a lot of writers who teach in college. I have never heard of one who came across a good manuscript and said to the hopeful applicant, "A university education would be deleterious to your natural-born talent. Avoid us like the plague." No one says that because their job is to make money, not good writers and not good writing.

Don't get me wrong. I think writing workshops and programs can be of great use to the fledgling writer. You get to meet other writers at pretty much the same level. You're able to exercise your voice. You meet people who care about writing and might know ways for you to hone your skills and maybe even get a few pages out there in the professional and public eye. Hey, that's a good start.

But remember: the university doesn't own you or your professor's writing; it doesn't own Shakespeare either. You should never pay more than the experience is worth. And you aren't becoming a writer so that you might one day be a teacher.

What people, institutions, and economic systems expect should not define you. Break it down. Figure out what is best, not for you but for your writing. Get in those three hours every morning. Eschew expectations. Do what you have to do to survive, all the while knowing that if the soul of your desire does not survive, the body loses meaning.

Putting It All Together

Beginning. Middle. End. This is story in its simplest form—from *once upon a time* to *happily ever after*. The story imposes a sense of order on the world. It ignites the imagination, bringing readers to places that not even the author could have imagined beforehand. It, the story, appears to us as one thing and slowly becomes something else; like a baby becoming a person, a person becoming distinct, a hope that was so beautiful that even the fact that it is dashed fills us, readers and writer, with melancholy and gratitude.

In order to get to this revelatory place we have to become storm hunters chasing after a thing that will overpower us, dismiss us, surpass us in every way. There is no weapon we can use to tame this force, no war to be won. We cannot defeat the storm, and so we have to accept that it will conquer us again and again until finally we become its thrall.

Only in this position of servitude can we infiltrate the soft and subtle susurrations of whispering story in the frictions between the unimaginably powerful and invisible gusts and gales of the cyclone.

Beginning. Middle. End. A noire reprise.

beginning

I met her in a bar. Don't get the wrong idea. She was beautiful, yes, and a little tawdry, I suppose. But her smile said, "Come here and buy us a drink, you poor fool."

middle

The guy standing next to her was at least a head taller than any other man in the room. When he saw me he glowered and his hands clenched into fists that would have put Sonny Liston to shame.

"Hi," the woman said. "I'm Doris. This here's my friend Pitt."

end

Pitt was dead and I was three shades past drunk. The woman calling herself Doris still had that sad smile on her lips; a smile that could not be removed or bargained with. A smile that said, "Sure, I know you," then added, "but so what?"

The above are the contours of that mile-wide tornado descending on the Great Plains farmer. But simply seeing the storm does not define it. Hating or fearing or even loving this assault of nature makes no difference. The only thing our farmer can do is to attempt, in her way, to survive the onslaught. This is character in action. This is where we find out who she is and how she will grow to endure or perish.

So, rather than a crude outline or flowchart, the structure of the story is an elemental rampage ripping apart the mundane reality of watching crops grow, children grow, parents growing older. Maybe survival is an iron bathtub that resists the winds, or the clawing, bloody fingers of a grandsire who feels alive for the first time in decades.

The structure is more complex than the conscious mind can fully contain, but that doesn't prevent the writer (and subsequent readers) from conjuring the fictive world out of the depths of our imaginations.

The blank page is synonymous with the blind fear that we might not survive the blitz. And the aftermath is where we see what our characters and their world are made of—the first step of rewriting. The composition of that world is cowardice and heroism, promises and lies, unexpected generosity and despair so profound that it outweighs the wages of love.

The novel isn't all fury and lust. There are ideas and concepts too. The novel is of primal intelligence, but first and foremost it is a passionate, instinctual thing.

One or more narrators tell the tale. The story itself is composed of language that forms into a coherent Voice. Characters come and go, commenting on what the narrative claims and what the author thinks. Signposts, images, and dialogue interrupt to break the oppression of certainty that the narrative voice of the story strives to impose.

All of this comes together in a physical world that houses, hounds, and propels the story through the characters and their attempts to find meaning in this mostly insouciant landscape. Describing this material environment challenges the writer, because it is, as far as human senses are concerned, limitless. We have to choose just the right props and places to enhance, reflect, and embody the passions unleashed.

Once these emotions rise to the surface we must describe them too. This is no mean feat because love is not love and hate not hate. Every ping and pull of the human heart has a unique vibration and needs to be understood, as far as possible, in its own terms.

Everything that has gone before comes to the writer through physical and emotional experience in the real world. Our world comes in riding on all our senses, but it goes out exclusively in words. The only tool we writers have is our ability to make words into the simulacra of complex experience that readers then convert through their own unique personality and intelligence.

That conversion brings us to poetry.

There was a young man named Nathan who attended my high school. He had moderate learning disabilities and emotional problems too. Nathan did not always have the words to express himself, and so he often used pantomime to answer questions or to make requests. On the lunch court some of the kids would ask Nathan questions to see what kind of contortions he might use to answer. These questions were often unkind but he never seemed to mind.

One day I heard someone ask, "What about the sun, Nathan?"

He gave a rare frown, then bent his knees and hunched over them with his hands hanging down before him. Then, slowly, he stood up, his arms rising above his shoulders as he rose. When he was fully erect his fingers splayed and his arms had formed a ninety-degree arc above his head. He smiled broadly, grinned actually. His face flushed with joy. It was, without a doubt, the most beautiful thing I ever saw in high school.

The poetry in Nathan was so strong that it survives, at least a little, even just in these words. Our novels would be lucky to have his knack. I knew that his understanding of the question, and of the sun, and his feelings about both were the answer to a query that did not understand itself.

Our novel passes through a deep cave, serenaded by the echoes of every voice it contains. These voices do not end their reverberations until a while after the story is over. And so, when the first words we read are "Call me Ishmael," we will know that name and hear it up to and even after the end of the novel. There are other names and characters, places and fears we hear, over and over, through the piece. There's Ahab and Queequeg, Moby Dick and the cook, harpoons and a quest that is hopeless, hopeless, hopeless.

These names, places, ideas, and fears blend into a mood broken only now and then to allow the reader, and the characters, to breathe a little. This mood, this underlying vibration, is the soul of our novel. It needs to be studied and sculpted, interpreted and rewritten as many times as it takes to make the patter and the pattern into a living thing.

* * *

Writing your novel is a seemingly endless, tumbling reflection of metaphor and red-blooded characters, of folly and happenstance and tragedy that is felt. It will frustrate and elate you. If you approach it with confidence and humility it might even teach you something.

The purpose of this book has been to show by example and intention how deeply you can go into your mind, excavating a world worth the struggle, the many thousands of hours, and just the right words.